Love's Invitation
and Other Works

Love's Invitation and Other Works

Simple Spiritual Journeying

THOMAS JOHN LEWIS

RESOURCE *Publications* • Eugene, Oregon

LOVE'S INVITATION AND OTHER WORKS
Simple Spiritual Journeying

Resource Publications
An Imprint of Wipf and Stock Publishers
199 W. 8th Ave., Suite 3
Eugene, OR 97401

www.wipfandstock.com

PAPERBACK ISBN: 978-1-6667-8940-9
HARDCOVER ISBN: 978-1-6667-8941-6
EBOOK ISBN: 978-1-6667-8942-3

11/26/24

To the Virgin of Guadalupe, Mexico

Pray, hope and don't worry. Worry is useless. God is merciful and will hear your prayer.

St Pio of Pietrelcina

CONTENTS

CONTENTS

ACKNOWLEDGMENTS

I need to thank God, The Father, The Son and The Holy Spirit.

Our Most Blessed Lady.

The Communion of Saints.

My wife Anna.

My Dad, Alan.

My sister Mary and my brother Anthony.

My good friend, Mr. Benedict Dybowski.

LOVES' INVITATION

when the trumpet and bells sound, in a momentary percussion-
  less cry
then the birds will flock down and sit motionless, restraining
  desire to fly

I will gather your children to me, all to me and I'll wipe all your
  tears away
for the lark and the robin and the cockerel, are not starving in my
  hands

moving with shadows and lights in a range, I sing as I wander and
  proclaiming, I dance
because all of life's mysteries suddenly open to me, as I am cov-
  ered by shadow of wings

there is a loneliness inside the human heart and mind and indeed
  within man's spirit
and I see I will understand nothing at all, if I cannot carry and
  fall, with the weight of everything in it

so I do and I dance and I find that I'm free, as I write and I pen an
  old song
written with love's only word and the best that I've heard, at my
  end please do sing along

FOREVER DREAMING

there is such a thing as beauty
and I see, I am not blind, blinded by love or by some mask
that I weave upon your face, with the threads of my mind

you are of the divine, an interwoven tapestry of delighting green
    meadows
formed by pressure, as to like diamond birthing
clasped and tightly in the mighty fist of God

Your hair is a caress, caressing faces that are both reading and
    writing
an invitation to a wedding feast, where a lamb leaps within those
    green meadows
and is the delight of its shepherd boy guarding

your lips are not like pomegranates to me and yet they are like
    pomegranates
that is, to him, that one, of me, that sees your beauty so clearly
as when the colors give joy, at the heights that birds can only
    dream of

my hope soars there you see, born by currents of surging heart
    and not air
and yet moving ever upward and free
to rest in a serene and godlike descent, onto the mercies of your
    breasts

they are like hills, lamb-laden and peaked by grace

grace like the clouds that form angels faces

that are simply dreams, given license to trespass upon reality

there on those hills, I am as at home as is the lamb

and I see the angels there, within those green meadows

as my reality becomes a dream, upon peaks now kissed by clouds
freshly finger-painted

as the fist of pain, becomes that of the shepherd boy, opening to
touch

and those angels faces, they smile at me and dream with me and
kiss

and with me, breathe in the fragrance, of the reality of 'forever
dreaming'

THE EYES OF THE ONE I LOVE

the eyes of the one I love are golden
and crazy, like all power and possibility
the infinite contained, within a man meek and small made
by himself alone and for my sake only

the eyes of the one I love are true, absolute and daring
and they shout, much like desperation
wanting and willing
for they are every type of adventure, instantly

the eyes of the one I love are demanding
my trust and my surrender
to come and see
so that where he is, there would I also be

the eyes of the one I love have cried
and they glisten now but with invitation
and with dreams of exhilaration, new realities for Himself and me
to ride and free, on the wings of His Spirit

the eyes of the one I love are beautiful
coloured, but not of this world
a palate of the present and the future you see, the eternal situation
when richer than the depths of ocean, I will know Him as He
   knows me

the eyes of the one I love are mine
not in my own head but simply to gaze upon
and to be completed by that gaze
as it reveals the true sum, of all of my questions

the eyes of the one I love have searched, all and everywhere
and have chosen to finally rest on myself, the very same reason he
  died
and from within the fire of his comely furnace
comes my bidding and yearning to be purified

the eyes of the one I love are impossibility in action
the once dead and now alive
the absolute infinity now containable
and containable only, within the eyes of the one I love

I SEE YOU, HOLY SPIRIT

I see you Holy Spirit, in the eyes of the blind, and the lame and
   the lonely
you are rare, looked for by some—and to me, I say I thank you
   and only

I trust you Holy Spirit, I do know that you are
with me a lamb's breath and a calling of name by maternal lips
   and gentle bosom

Holy Spirit, quite often I know your breathing, in lungs of smiling
   exhalation and peaceful
the drawing and dawning of love's own dream awakens

SPARKS

There is always a risk in adventure
and adventure is our way
and the only way is to be filled and to be affected
by the sparks of life

most people never ignite
but I am a blazing furnace
tumbling in exultant joy, down banks of fertile creativity
and to be certainly realised vision

I invite you to kindle
to prepare your soul
to touch the spark that I am
ever so gentle and yet vibrant

Come and find in adventure
the knowing of answers
and the experience of ideas
conceived and birthed into flame and into life

and let the spark within you
become adventure's beacon
calling siren-like to dormant stars
our celestial-like brothers and sisters

ignite and grow, my friend
risk all and know
your genius
and your self

THE GIVING OF MAN AND WOMAN

To me and to my universe, you are the rule, the center and the face
god-speeded light, as a dancing invitation to good and to dream
in the knowledge of expectations true and attainable
for the light has already reached my eye and my heart
and warms the patterns of my brain and mind and hope

Heaven is in your smile; within your eyes, the angels wink at me
   unmolested
purpose is given sinew and flesh and movement given to my
   bones to ideal destination
that carpeted hearth of touch and ecstatic sleep and racing adven-
   ture all combined
in embrace and tear and lips, in caress and gift and peace
the giving of man and woman

THE RABBIT AND THE DOVE

The rabbit grimaced as it fell into the trap once more
it was his last leg gone now
one other one and one other one, went in before
fighting was his game and boy he was game and didn't he know it
for to himself in the trap and to his own bloody lips
own flesh, yet tasting the same

The dove can be, a reckoning all majesty
along the borders of the pretense to be familial
never a judge, never a judge
was the cry of the lamed, all uttered through gritted teeth and
    blood sweating
just wait and see, just wait and see
the wings serenade and with graceful energy beat

The rabbit flew along and almost crashed but not quite
stopping a fair few inches short of what might have been another
    long-lasting lesson
he was faster now, without the strength of limb he'd always knew
(and only through grim, brotherly tolerance)
for giving him flight, was another brother and a far more gracious
    lover
everything pure in his mind

some revelations of love are written at night
on blankets of perpetual warmth of a sunlight
devastation and cessation are considered as one
and are equal to dawning of said very sun
but surely all creatures below and all creatures above
are enveloped in blankets warmed, but by sweet breaths of fair
    heavenly dove

MOUNTAINS

Mountains, they are massive, that's what I say
for they almost decide and then force you to pray
they can plane and intimidate you, leaving you fear dusted
in awe and yet tantalized, moved and mysteriously
moved by the raw, by the majesty and grace
the time chiseled jaw and flint-set face
Just a spectacle of size and stoned muscle
challenging one to get in the ring with the king and to wrestle
    with him
whether I conquered or not, I would gain respect
at least in respect of my own brutish possibilities
though I have never climbed, no I very well might have died
I say this in my own defense, for I am seeking your deference
and perhaps my own innocence, from any hint of cowardice
though the reason is not that simple for I am a sensitive man, and
    I don't like heights
that and though it's not easy to say but you shouldn't find a sinner
any sort of a sinner, up there that high, on any given day
it's not easy to say, as I have managed to say
but there is more, that I would like to say
there is beauty with the power and radiance with the still
the dead still, but with potentials own life
ever mammoth in its penetrating eye
and ever eyeballing one with some stupendous sigh
a very simply stated 'come on, do or die'
and then quivers down the spine, as I do in mine
and questions that echo, that echo in the mind

but I am kind, kinder to myself, than to simply go

just for facing's sake or for saving face for that matter

but I would put my hands upon that wall

and look up and begin, not caring should I fall

for that's what it takes, I believe when I think

it is freedom from fear and from life's chilling whisper: 'you
would lose me forever'

but yes, when I am ready and perhaps when I am bidden, I will
climb, Mountains

JESUS' BOOT

The feet are heavy
walking here and there
to and fro
and heavy, as you know

sometimes they stop
and I see my friends
working quite as hard
as we protect and bend

I've served this master
for quite some time
I hear many noises
the laugh and of course, the cry

I see a crowd
along the way
sometimes at night
but almost always in the day

I have brothers here
that talk with me
that are strapped as well
to their traveler's feet

yet I cannot say
that I understand
for my recent discourse
was never planned

and when I say
my friends offer me their prayer
it's what I imagine
not what I can hear

for I never true
could talk before
I just didn't think
all this or anything more

It's all become
a strange reality
for without any eyes
I can honestly see

so whenever did it start
when did I get a beating heart
I think it was along the way
that awesome moment, on that awesome day

when Jesus' feet were put in me
that's when I did begin to see
and I remember being told
cry out young thing and just be bold

for the people, they will cease their cry
when on a hill your master dies
but you be hardy and be well stout
give a heartfelt sigh and then wholly shout

the master I serve
and you must know the truth
is the son of God
I am alive and still only, Jesus' boot

POETRY

Poetry is not written so much by poets
as by its resonance
the words have a life and a desire for union
as do all men and works of same

real people and real emotion
dancing with each other while examining other's feature
I cannot believe a half of what I read is dancing
more like writhing all but naked, on the page

criticism is a tool and a surgeon's knife
wield not at all if the aim isn't life
go to the closet and sit in the dark
and move mountain with your will, only then

I am not pretending to be a saintly man
or a sinner beyond the dawn of hope's beacon
only a friend to weaklings and to the lovers of beauty
for we are the same in the final exchange

romancing and romance and many a better line plenty
escape me but find me and make me a better man
gracefully reading what is gracefully wrote
remember one's mother and float, little boat

A REAL MAN

My father is a man and a real one
as well as being divine and well-intended

he makes mistakes though, at least in this life
for I am now describing the human element and not the inside

mysteries can unravel one but before they ever unravel
the understanding of a diamond is to let in the light

all clarity is perhaps a gentle reminder of each small ecstasy given
when love's kind moment decides the time is now right

I haven't forgotten all that you've done, not the work, not the fun
there is a purpose to my pain and I know that you are in no way
    to blame

moreover, you are a hero in my eyes and I do not tell you a lie
there is more to you than simply the salt, which makes tears of
    my eye

Father and father, in the end will be one
and I know in the end I will still be God's son

but I stand here before you, though only words do you hear
in your mind and perhaps alone

remember Dad that I told you, before it occurs
that we will wrestle again, when you at last do come home

FRIENDSHIP

Friendship breathes fire into the cold and impossible places
hidden recesses, where pain stills with its icy talons, fixed and
  forcing
forcing agonies untold and uninvited
and tortures lucid
yet deliriously meant and meaning

feel, cries the friend
feel my arms and neck and breath, breathe in and feel
and oh, but to feel, in the moment when all seems lost
to tenderness and to hope
in a vacuum of loss that sucks black eyed and dead eyed

It is more than a light coming on unexpectedly, in the abyss of a
  dark room
some dark cell, a prison of one's own passions and promises
a car crash of dreams and desire
now broken bodied with spilled blood and guts and filth
a bad dream in a death perfumed nursery

So be a friend, turn on the light
let it shine and let it touch
let the memory of your love, become more immediate and in the
  moment than time itself
and let it grow and develop into fidelity
as to the impossibly great man behind the veil

RAYS OF MERCY IN THE MORNING RAINBOW

We are always in the fields and we gather
we gather enough for the day and then we play
in the light that the sunlight is only a part of

promising and finding that reasons of perpetuity
are closing in all around you
gives a nuance to the greatness of the call on your heart

there are times ahead in life that we must all face
and we all face them, but not in union do we stand
before the mighty judgement seat of God

given and received are the lights from the sunlight
each one a fine example of what draws us to hope
we are not alone in the rainbow

I am only absent when I am hated
so, find me again and find me again and let parodies cease
I am a traveler here and I am not going to stop on the road

when the fresh grass breathes all through the night
I walk there and I run there, and I am satisfied, redemption is not
    beyond me
and I look up and I wait for the sun to arise

I LOVE YOU—A POEM

I live for you and I die for you
and I always will
until that day of death, becomes my forever letting go
and I can pour my cauldron of self and of distrust, pain and hate
into the chalice of Gods' own blood

what fiery quench will one day
warm the very limits of our eternal ambition
to wholly satisfy that now dreadful obsession
for love and for home
and we can forever own the knowing, of 'I love you'

MAN'S INNOCENCE

I have never been able to love
not as I ever, ever wanted to

I am only young, and I find that all of

my dreams lay in front of me
not one single, behind

I could be compared to the small gem one finds
in a ring on the finger of a resolute child

I am unseen and all but unknown and I'm so grateful to know
and to be conscious of my own deep inadequacy

the only delight of my life, is my life and I call her by name
'Innocence', she is free and bold and I need to tell her so

goodness doth labor for me and it carries a heavy burden
but I have desired all things for love

ANGELS—A POEM

Angels are deliberate and exacting beings
they are as thunderous as power can be in perfection
and as gentle as one single snowdrop in flight
alighting from an early spring breeze
they enlighten the sky at night, as claim some
they tell earth's story
and the story of love
constellations as an indication, of the heaven to come

Michael is their prince
a grace-hearted warrior sure
who is like unto God
his cry with love's victory power
Michael's eyes, they see and perceive
and with angelic will, he fights for thee
he draws hell's might and humbles it
down-crashing to the knee

Gabriel is a melody,
a most mild and charming sound
good news he brings and when he sings
all Heaven's joy abounds
Gabriel, I should fear to grieve
by not heeding his word
Zachariah mute and long
surely you have heard

Raphael is a medicine
and a balm from above
his sword, it is healing
with the mysteries of love
Raphael knows your pain
and is aware of your plight
your prayer, permits heaven's command
for his wings to take flight

So, angels are warriors
messengers and both in the one
they fight and they fly
within a battle now won
they whisper of better times
putting thoughts in our mind
and with truth-fragranced breath
remain forever and kind

MOMENTS OF MADNESS

moments of madness come passing me by in the street sometimes
disguised as gentlemen, they politely doff their hats
I am caught in a trap, bounders one and all
I pretend that I haven't caught their eye and that that will be that

remember when you see a friend, along the paths of life's long
    morning
that in the eventide he may be coming back along the same way
not everyone is a chancer, but I have been
though it's not the right time, twilight, to play a game, with no
    distant light from the moon

Madness!
Reaching out, I call her name and I try to pick a fight, she doesn't
    hear me
when suddenly, the see-through dress she is wearing proves to be
    an optical illusion
In the end not a disappointment, for she is a lot older than I am
    and a better fighter than me

peculiarities have consequences in the invitations that one receives
and pretentious speech is envious of sun rays and happy days and
    all things are in the mire of it
my desire is for transparency, I used to say to my mother
on evenings when falling from trees was the only way home

THE REALITY OF DELUSION—A POEM

The loss, is as that of a child
not the raw emotional pain but deep and dark defeat
the child, my hopes and dreams
the life promised and yet not
believed and yet forsaken in a quake of reality, alien and booming

woe, woe! is the cry of my heart now
drowned in a torrent of light as dark as pitch
in air, clear and breathable as some transparent tar
what an intrigue and what a joke
and only devils are laughing

I am a punchline
a murdered and consumed line
cocaine esq' in the nose of the evil one
while the fire and death are all in my own veins
coursing and coarsening

Reality has become a mockingbird
a jester of pale and yet vibrant deceit
and now I am a beggar, picking through its garbage heap
looking for a pearl of great price, that yesterday I had thought mine
yet today, I see as a washer and not worth

I ask, what now and why
I dispense with the why, a vain attempt at hope
and a hope chain heavy and pendulum free, swinging around my
   neck
and dragging me down and down, to low places of humiliation
while I search madly at its end for a key

enslaved and entombed, I cry, acceptance is freedom, acceptance
   is freedom
but what cost this freedom and I a beggar
I am all but lost and yet I must hope
for death has her jaws open
and her breath is not heavenly scented

my heart and my head shake and my bones may too
before I find that key, the ethereally fantastic thing, truth
I mean the person and not some actor playing the part
I know, for I have leapt on the stage
only to look in the eyes of an imposter, God help me

He will, but even this somehow terrifies me
My brief loss has hurt Our Father too
the child, bruised blue and blue
—fostered for a time by death,
until Life cried out, My Son!

PERSPECTIVES IN PEACE

wonder has a reason for its conception
and it doesn't remember it

mercy falls on one in the morning dew
and alights in the drawing of a much kinder picture

kindness can create and can form the mind and the motions of life
bad emotions, dangers and hell's own triumph, it denies

hope is an angel like vessel and peace inside the turbulent mind
falling, calling and refusing to leave

the message of Jesus is the reason
I remember now

JUST FOR YOU, OH LOVELY—A POEM

he just waits there
the child doth cry
he just waits there
the mother sighs
always, always

What is he waiting for
the child's reply
just for you, oh lovely
the mother smiles
always, always

oh, does he not know
how this child has grown
and now seeks free
and how now, could never be
always, always

in truth and love
of course, he does
spend some time with him
and you will know he's still
always, always

pressure I feel
to bow and kneel
boredom I know
I just want to go
my friends the same
and it's you I blame
always, always

I will set you free
from bended knee
I shall let you go
but just same know
blame not mine to own
friend, just him alone
always, always

I am here, now speak
be not mild and meek
give me something real
let me know or feel
I cannot take this pain
why am I here again
why, once was said to me
right here, will you be
always, always

but I am here to speak
I am mild and meek
I am someone real
I know how you feel
I only, could take this pain
I brought you here again
for once you did say to me
right here will you be
always, always

with you I would not walk
when did you hear that talk
oh my God, I did not lie
response to mother's sigh
what, you did wait for me
I said 'no' to bended knee
own mother to blame did give
walked away and to live
lost both way and friend
grief, shame, pain no end
always, always

you are not alone
do not doubt, I own
the pain of which you spoke
the truth that you forsook
wait here now for me
bend heart and mind and see
own blame, no more to give
walk my way and live
friend, mother, all is me
just for you, oh lovely
always, always

THE LILY—A POEM

you are perhaps, an apparition
fresh, beautiful and pure
as no lily ever dared to aspire
yet nature's boast you are, its triumph
pristine 's own untouchable, your body
dignity's own condescension, your soul
always assuring my own scarred hands to liberty and to touch
to feel your delicacy and to inhale the fragrance of the center of you
to know you, your scent and purpose, to be with you
to hold and to behold you, the beauty of your shape and form
a higher perfection than petals, in angel 's wings similitude
bliss I find in your presence, watching you still and then moved
by breath, sweet as breeze blown gently from the poles of heaven
you close my eyes, drunk with satisfaction
I can sleep, I can awaken, I am no longer alone

REACHING OUT AND LETTING GO—A POEM

I am wondering about all the things that I have yet to say
and I do not yet know how to say them
it isn't that I have no voice or no mind
only that my reality can be very harsh, even unkind

judgement falls on the unsuspecting man
I suspect and I am only being myself
will you listen, will you hear me
and are you able to conceive of a time when we would be friends

The concept of the promise is one that I am conscious of
most early mornings alone, in the moonlight that I am graced
I have always been a fool and I am now looking to you
are you a better man than I am or are you an idiot, as he was

merciful trust is a necessary trembling within
and I tremble very much within, on these mornings
but my idiocy is not a contagion and I really wish it were
the trust that I have, is not my own and I am gifted in this respect

can I ask a question, would you ponder and listen
the finality of my condition moves me to the edge of reality
and here I am able to complete the circle
confidence in abandonment and in your heart, as my focus, as I fall

A MATTER OF LIFE OR DEATH—A POEM

Oh, how my heart aches
between the joy of you
and the death of me
yes, at all the pain of man

it is a strange reality
that I shed a tear
at every tear I hear
more than at those I see

but the word is he
which penetrates me
perhaps there is more truth in that
yes, certainly

many aches we have inside
our pain for those who've died
sorrow is in our blood
every sacrifice

I cannot begin to comprehend
without the understanding
of that poor man
and his first fall

into the dust of time
the winds of change did blow
all around this earth
its burial, to know

the end will surely come
creeping as it does
for day by day
its voice speaks silently

tomorrow is always a promise
yet some tomorrows are a curse
some strain of destruction's breath
behind the ear of Man

So onward we go
yet backwards we face
learning through our mistakes
we hope, I hope, for you

understand then man
fallen bloody man
renounce yourself and time
and face the death of thine

avoid forever naught
journey with hope sought
lost till now perhaps
but eternal in its offering

and forever in its finding
will be the salvation contained
and forever remained
within its clean breath of promise

salvation is an embrace
of death and loss
to find, through that cross
a new life of hope

A LADDER

Have a care
if you dare
to prepare
all is there
if you can see
and with me
what you really need to do

carry on
don't slow down
but don't be hasty
without purpose
and in the morning
give a cup
to the thirsty one

I am not
everyday
I can think
I can fail
but I rise
with a light
in the eye

Man is not
we are all
like children
in this fall
and I try
to convey
better times

you are
and I see
though I do
really see
it's not
anything
that you say

it's the way
that you smile
it's the look
in your eye
that is truly
what gives
you away

I have nothing
if I am
on my own
and I stand
not before
but along
by your side

keep it real
and so simple
give me time
and I will
find a notion
that can show
and convey

many days
and many times
they come
passing by
by the way
I fall
everyday

have a heart
read along
sing with me
you know the song
I'll begin
will you follow
simply hum

home and soon
that's the truth
fail to see
as you do
but we are
but a breath
in the wind

Adam came
and he saw
he was conquered
nothing more
and its time
to begin
rise again

for the sin
it was more
than sad
and low
but I know
that I have
sinned as well

THE SWAN—A POEM

The swan was discovered all on a thunderous morning
delighting and with the lightning, the eyes of the mourners

they were a tragedy and a parody of sincerity and care
'Oh, death where is thy victory' they sang not
their hearts were coarse and only 'aspects of love' they hummed,
    as they walked

forgotten are the embers of the fires of birth
when body motionless makes love to the earth

'I can think of no sadder sight to find on the way', said one, a
    paragon of virtue he was, back in the day
'All of life mysteries are contained in the Swan, I heard once', another
    man from Brighton beach trumpeted up with a resounding blast
'I've never subscribed to the truth and I'm not going to start now',
    said another

calamity, calamity and calamity more
the swan raised its head and with an eye full of pity
'I am sorry for you', it seemed to convey
through pools of deep water, eye now weeping away

many are the reasons and cares that kill and kill sure
but I am certain of this, that bad things do never endure

one more line, just for you, who is waiting for me
I'm the swan and I'm here, right now on the page. Can you see?

SUNDAY—A POEM

Sunday! what a day, it's so hard to say
whether I like it or not, it's a kind of grey
yet it is the Lord's Day, the day of rest, the day that's best
to honour our God, the one and only joy of man's desire
and the honest joy of any decent heart and mind

But I ask what kind, what kind of a man am I
if I can only find the boredom and not the freedom
to enjoy the rest and the other lack of stimulation
perhaps there is something wrong with me, in my heart and in
    my mind
because often I find that my heart is not in it

It seems to be a day with nothing to gain
but counting the drops of rain
that seem to be a falling on my head
though instead, I ought to say and it ought to be
a day of joy and a day of gaining experience of the one I love

My God, I want to cry and I want to die
a thousand deaths but all in ecstasy
and I want to soar and search the more
that I know there is, in Him for me
for no matter what I want to feel, I just get bored

When in the kneel, of the very wooden pew
listening to very wooden words of some very wooden man
that could simply be an oak
if that weren't a joke and it is
though not a very funny one

So, I've got to find some peace of mind
and purpose and reason
and I've got to understand
and in or out of season
My God, where are you on a Sunday

you can only imagine a day when all went quiet
and nothing else was really a riot
save the mirth that you heard
coming quite like a bird, gently across air
with its own news and current

and you can only imagine
that every single one was given over to this fun
and that in the eye, of every passer by
you could see a look
a look of love

and a look of love, so touching and so genuine
that you, yourself
wanted to leave everything
and that you really and truly wanted to follow
almost right now and not just tomorrow

and imagine too, that when the church bell rang
everyone got excited and everyone went silent
and then everyone went and everyone knelt
and prayed for each other
and not just their mother

and imagine again
when the man said the word
that Christ himself was the man that you heard
and imagine once more, that when you took the bread
Christ himself, was the one Christ that fed

and imagine when over, you knew you were in clover
and that you were grateful beyond
and in love, simply set free from hell's bond
and all of this bliss
well, it wasn't amiss

and imagine it was, because it just wasn't odd
because as everyone could
well, they did and did true
show that they knew
exactly, where God is, on a Sunday

WRITER'S BLOCK

reasons and reasons to write
dancing in the valley of the dark mind at night
how many more times am I going to stand out here alone
in the blinding light, surely you see

constantly and constantly re-reading my word
I 'm only half-joking and my humour is a thief in the night, long
    since gone
Cornelius, he knew it all didn't he
and I doubt if I can ever find a punchline

generally, I have more than enough but it's less than the hairs on
    my head
and they count for something
I pause: the day is half gone now and I am traversing bad weather
my coat is holy, as a net, I believe and yet I am still as dry as a
    bone

catatonic avenues of small roads and paths, on a map surely de-
    signed by Cornelius
I don't know if I can bother to identify the handle on it that I
    don't have
lucidity, morbid often, with grace behind me telling me to slow
    down
I look into the rear-view mirror and then shudder greatly, sud-
    denly at my journeys end

the patterns played games with me, telling me lies

truly, I am graven and an image that I must burn to the nothing

but I will not awaken Elijah

I will cast my cares upon the lord and suffer, laughing in the end
at myself

www.ingramcontent.com/pod-product-compliance
Lightning Source LLC
Chambersburg PA
CBHW051047030426

42339CB00006B/230